when life seems black n white...

make sure that you dream in

dream in

color

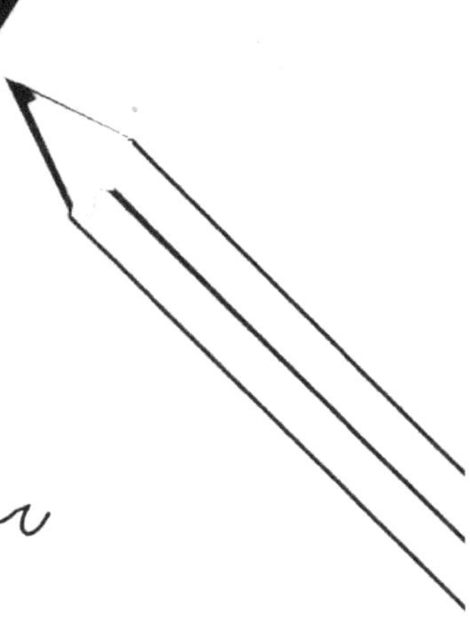

a book of illustrated quotes to color

by Christa Valente

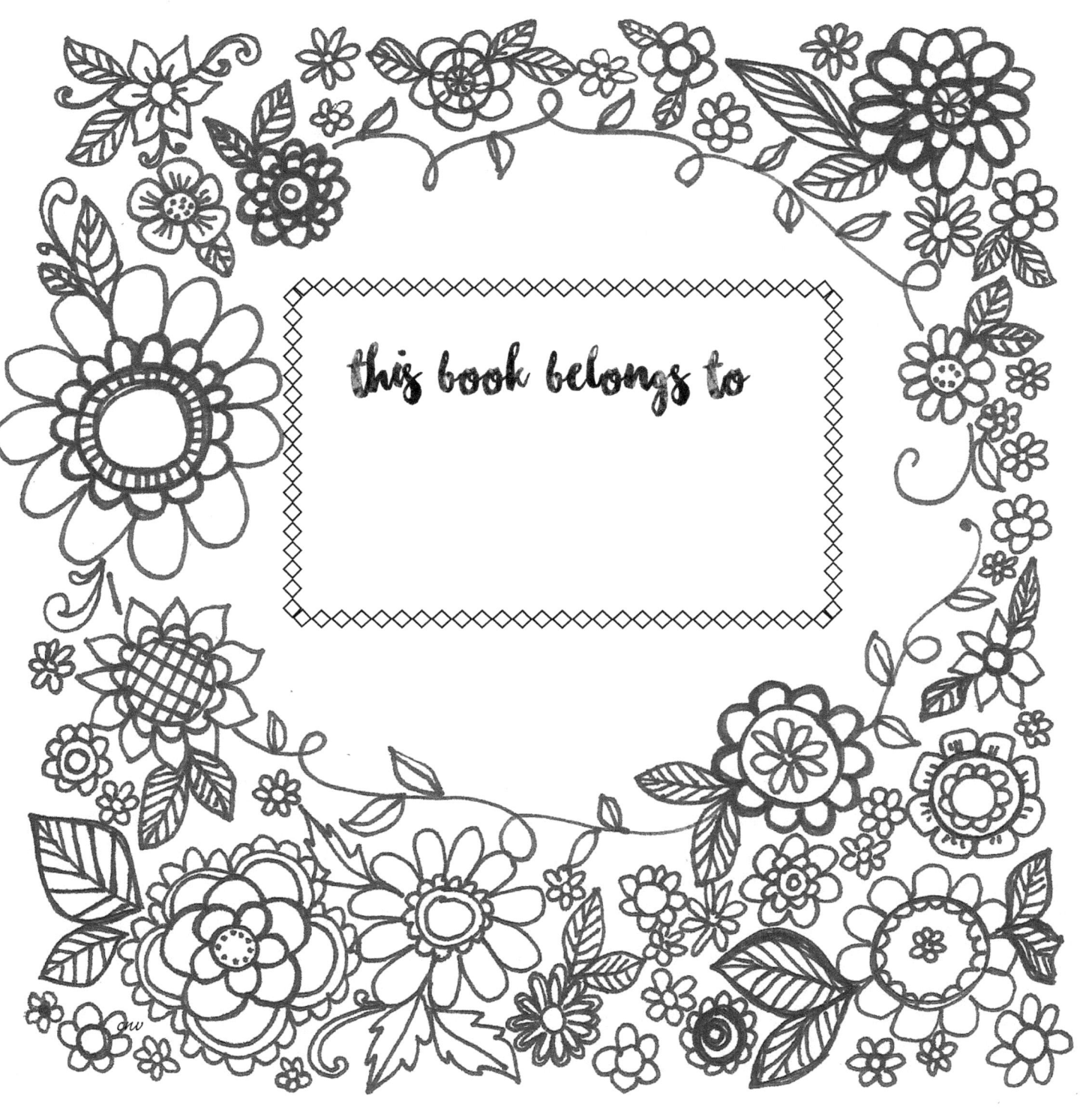

this book belongs to

tips for coloring

Colored pencils and gel pens are ~~my~~ favorite coloring utensils but you can use just about any materials to color the pages of this book.

If you use paint, Sharpies, or markes that could bleed, you may want to remove the page before you color it to avoid it soaking through, or place a piece of scrap paper between the pages to avoid any bleeding. The back of each page is intentionally left blank so if bleeding occurs it will not ruin a design on the reverse side.

color test page

Test your colors here and use it as a reference!

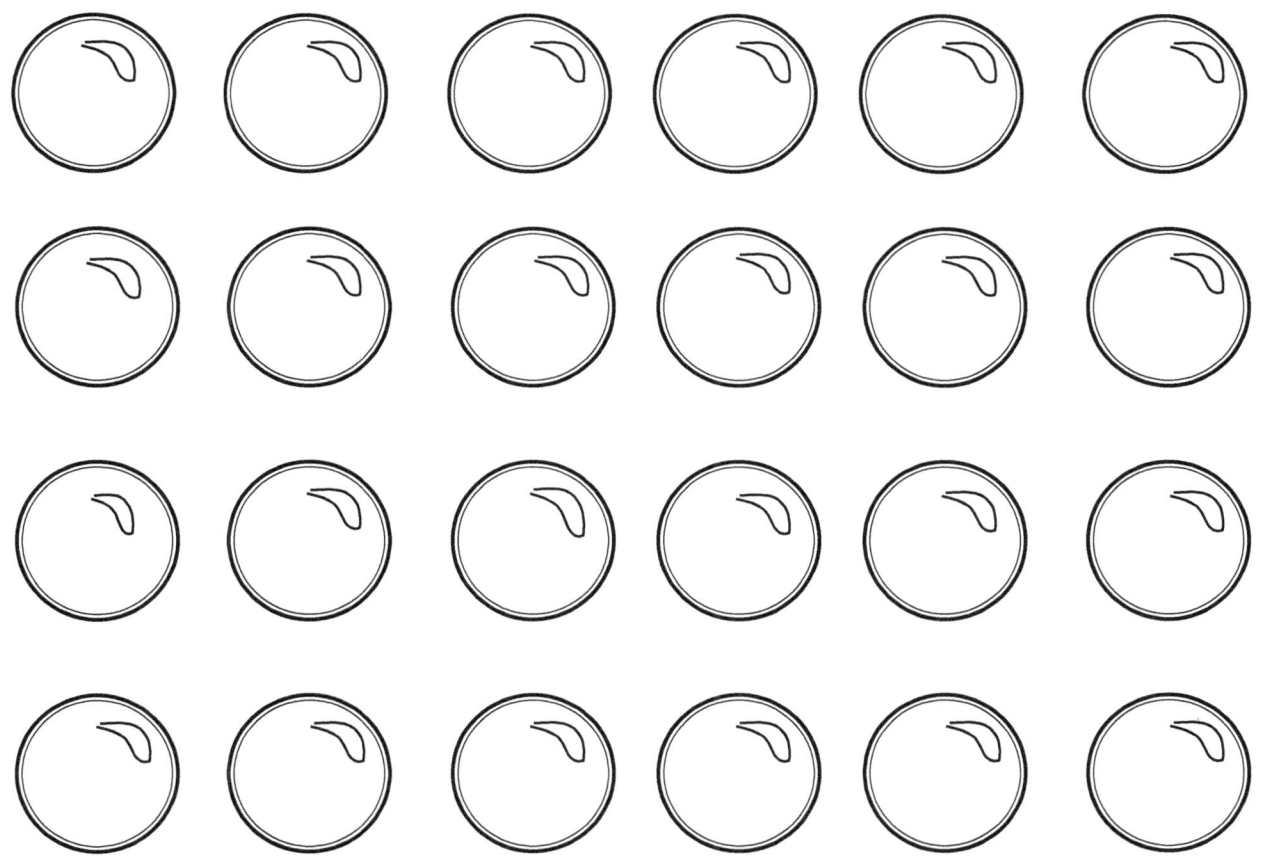

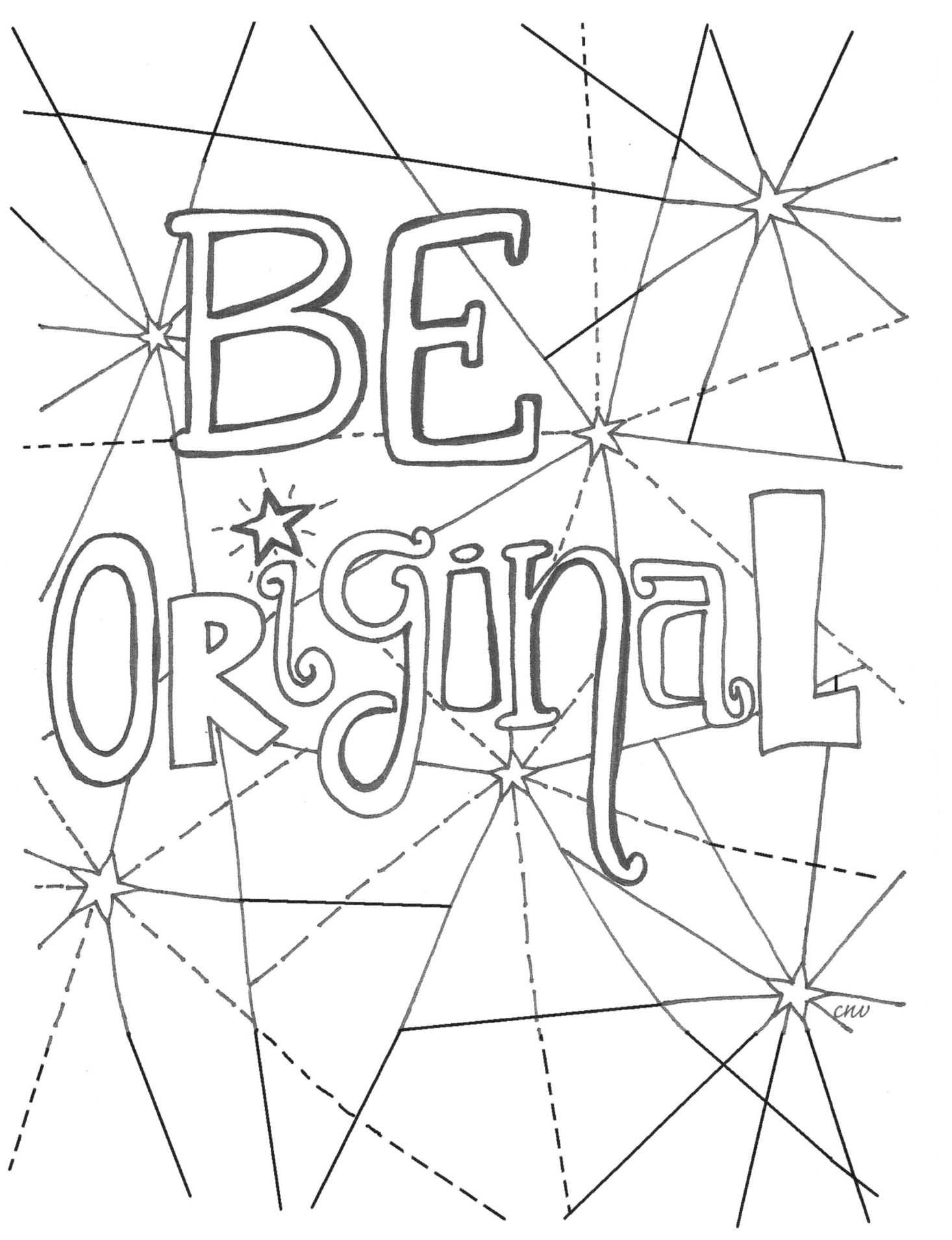

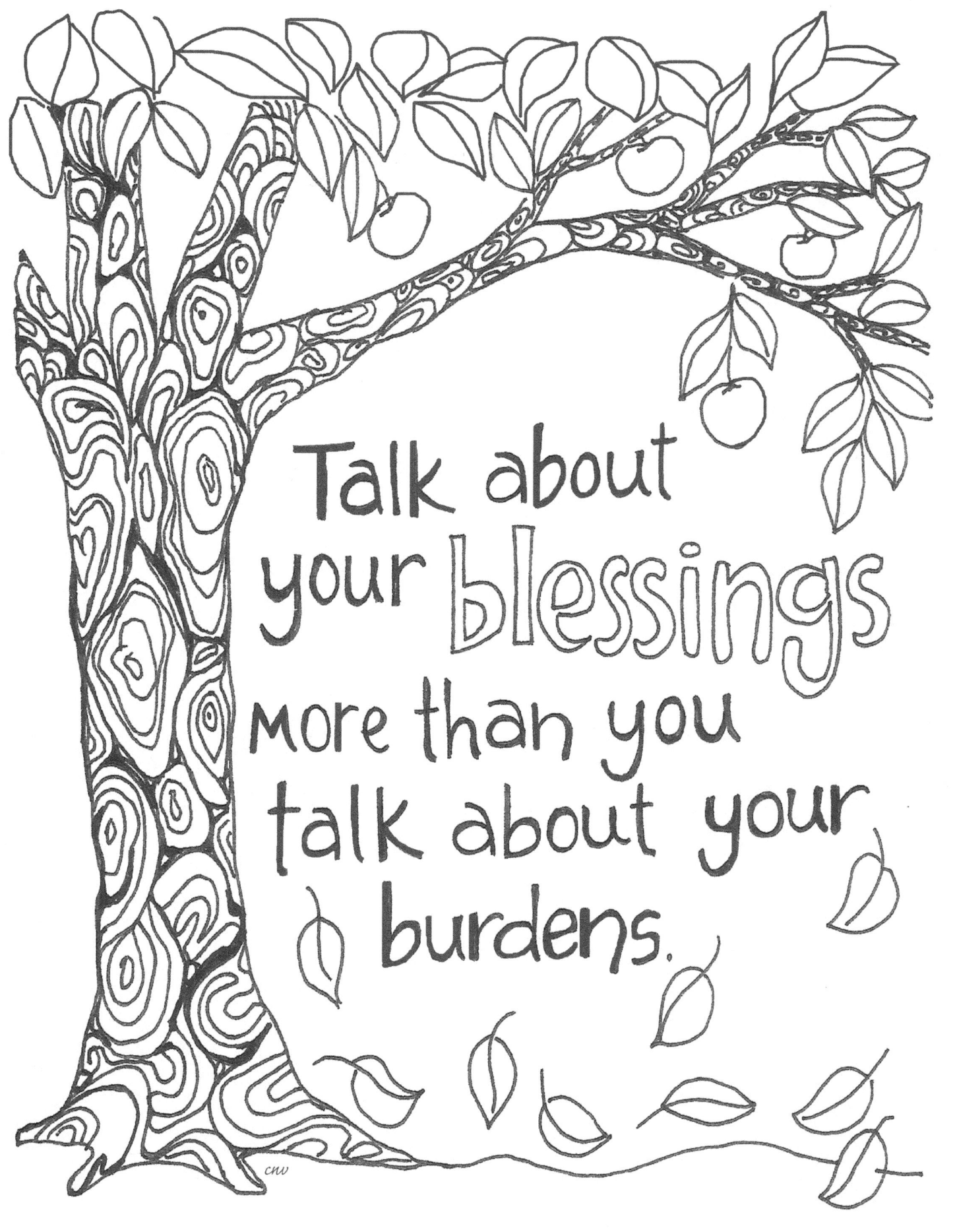

Talk about your blessings more than you talk about your burdens.

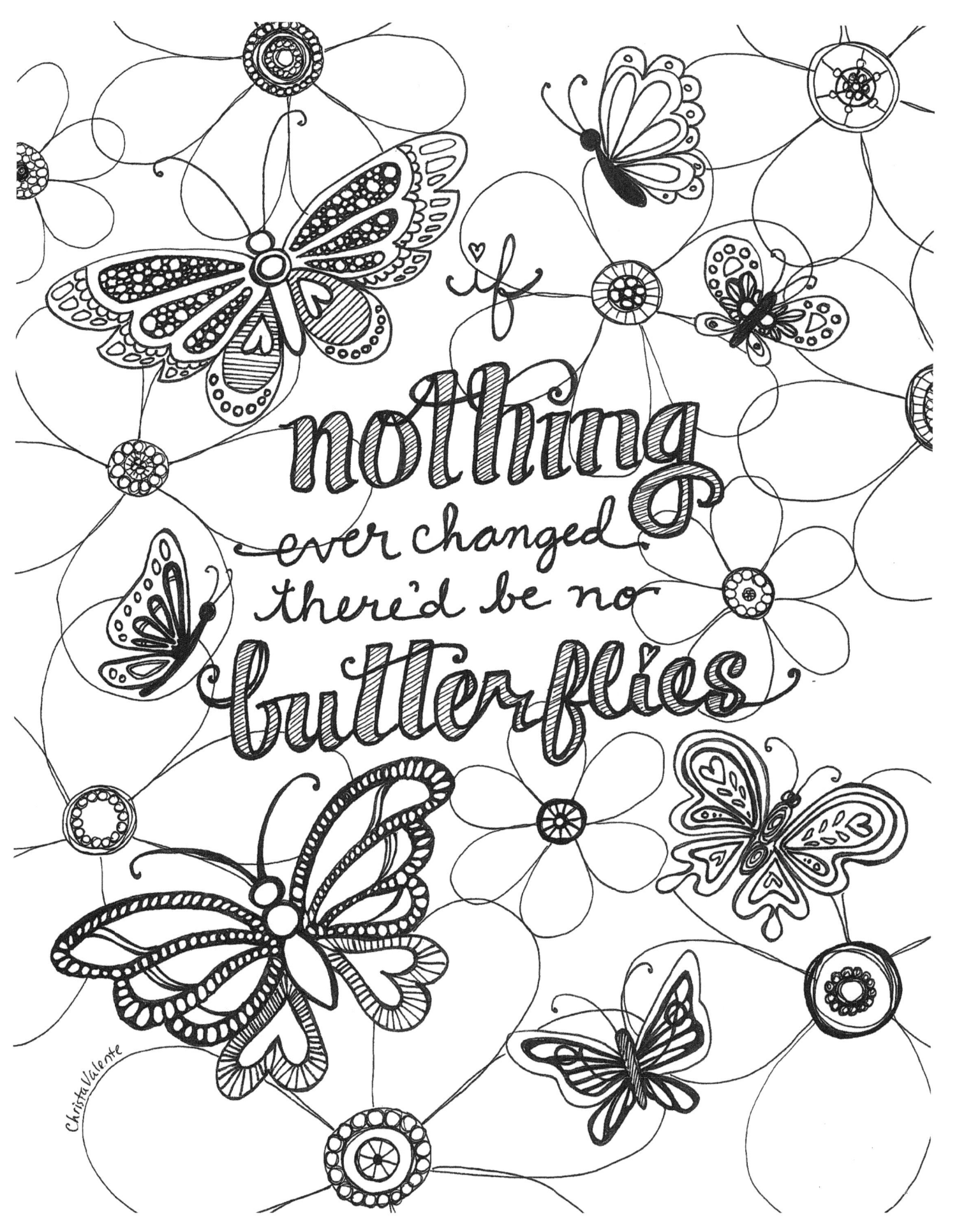

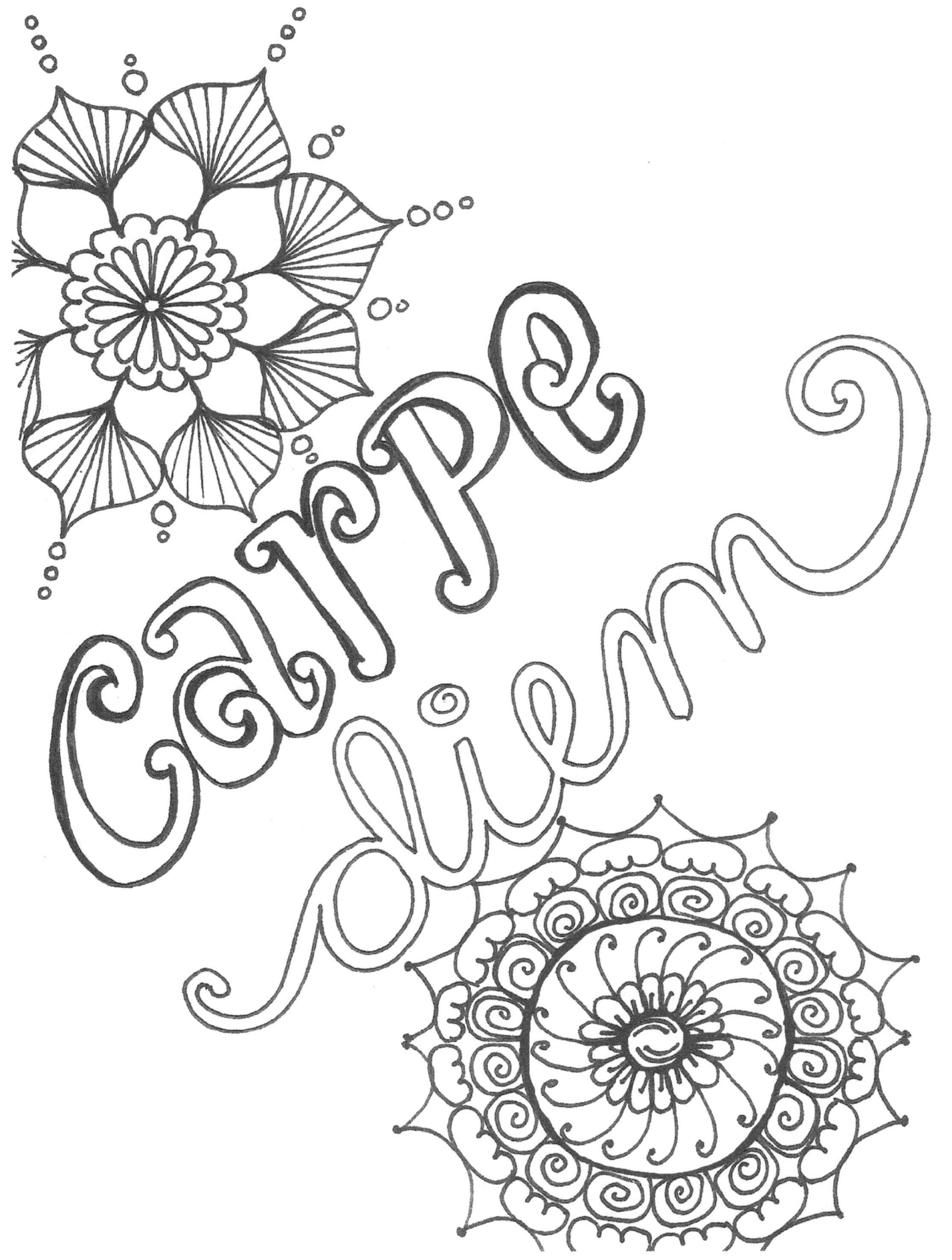

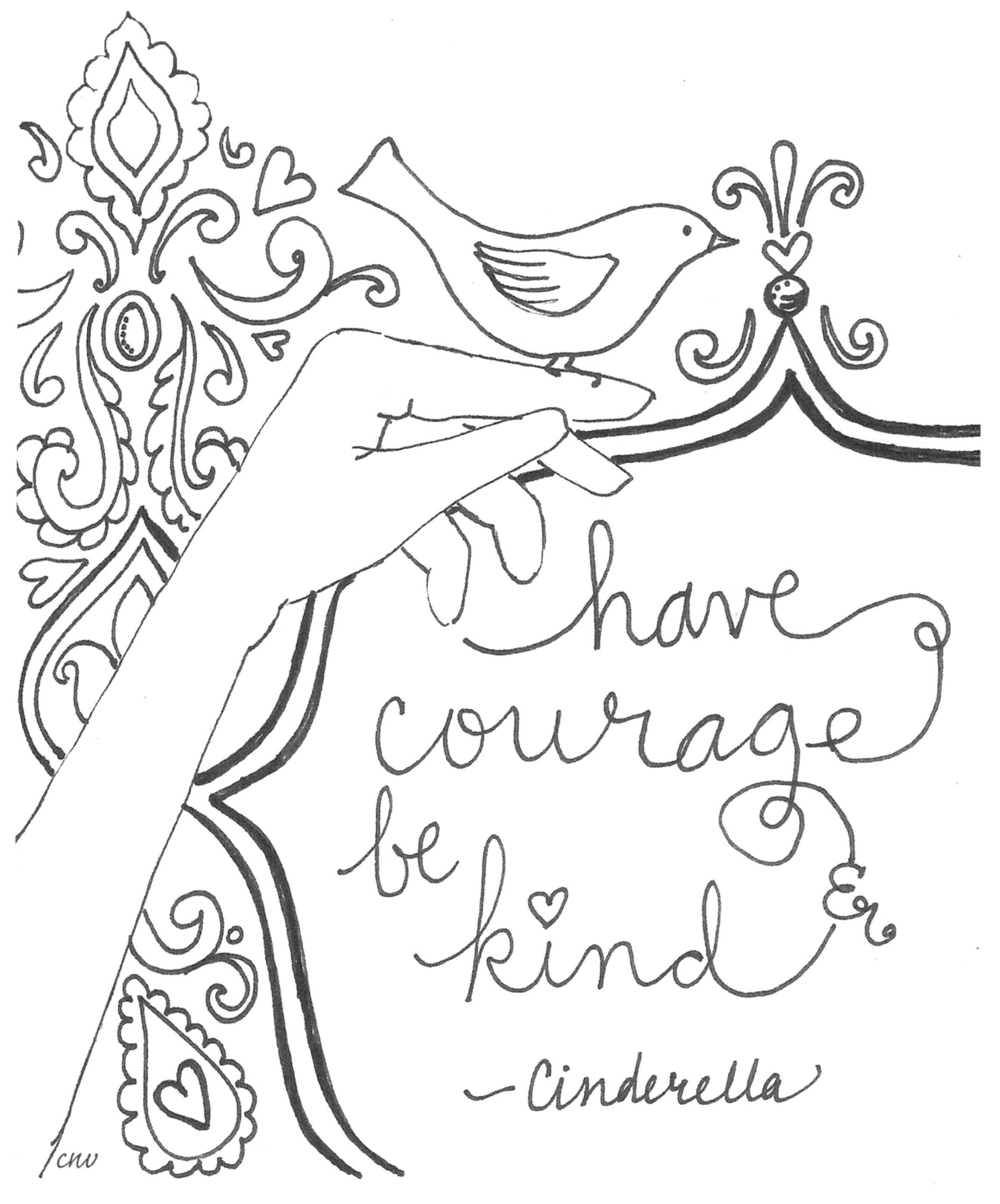

have
courage
be
kind &

—Cinderella

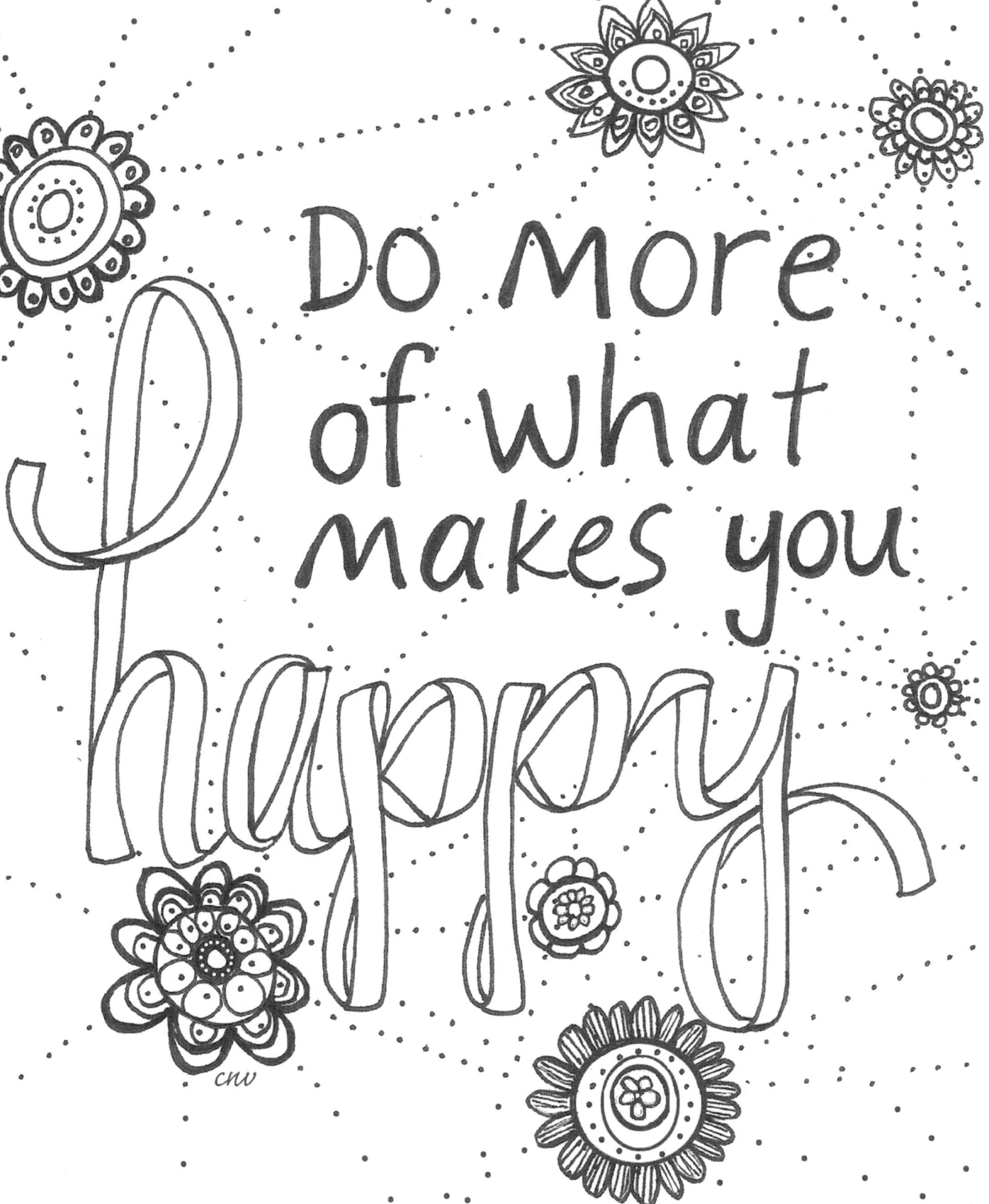

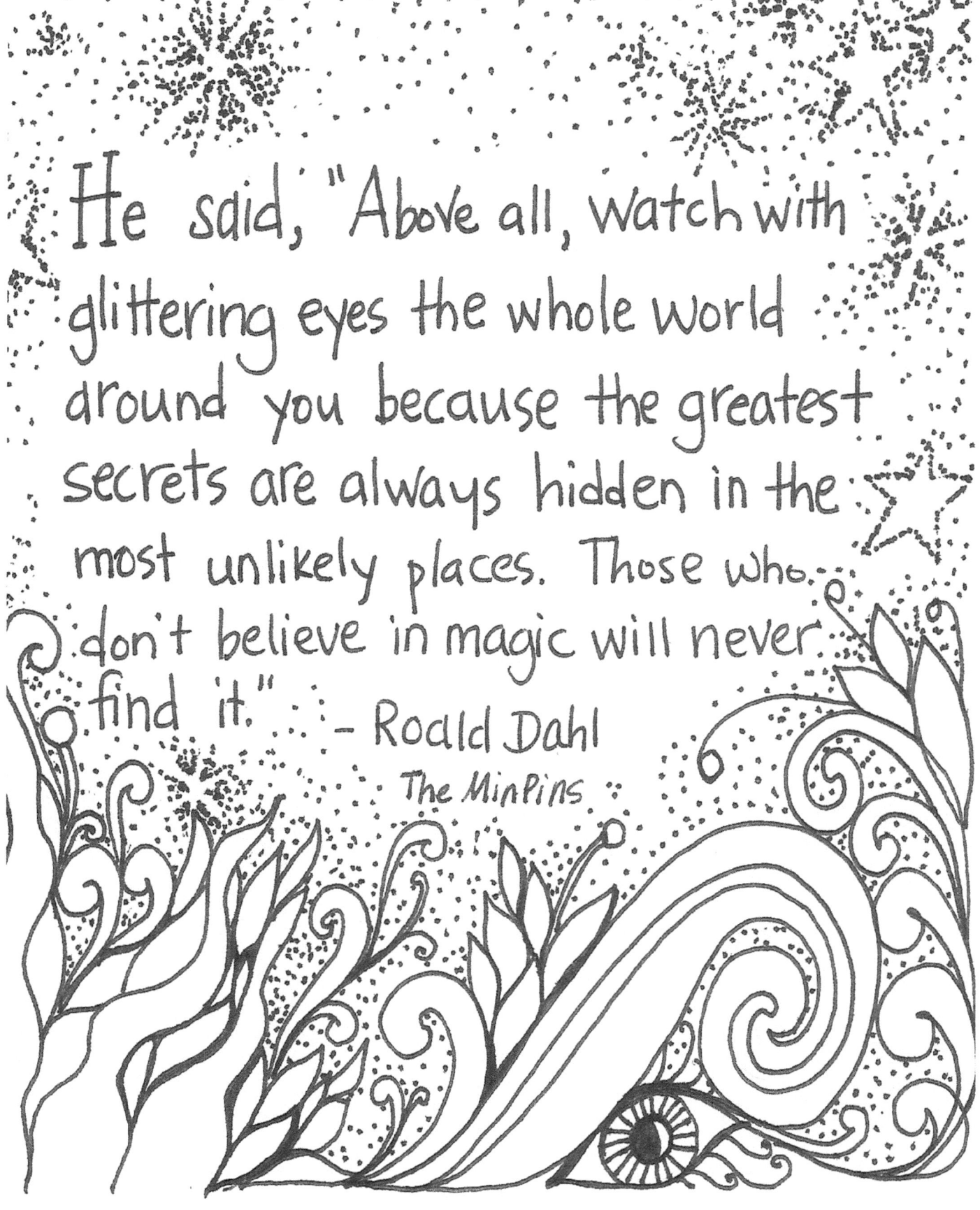

He said, "Above all, watch with glittering eyes the whole world around you because the greatest secrets are always hidden in the most unlikely places. Those who don't believe in magic will never find it."

– Roald Dahl
The MinPins

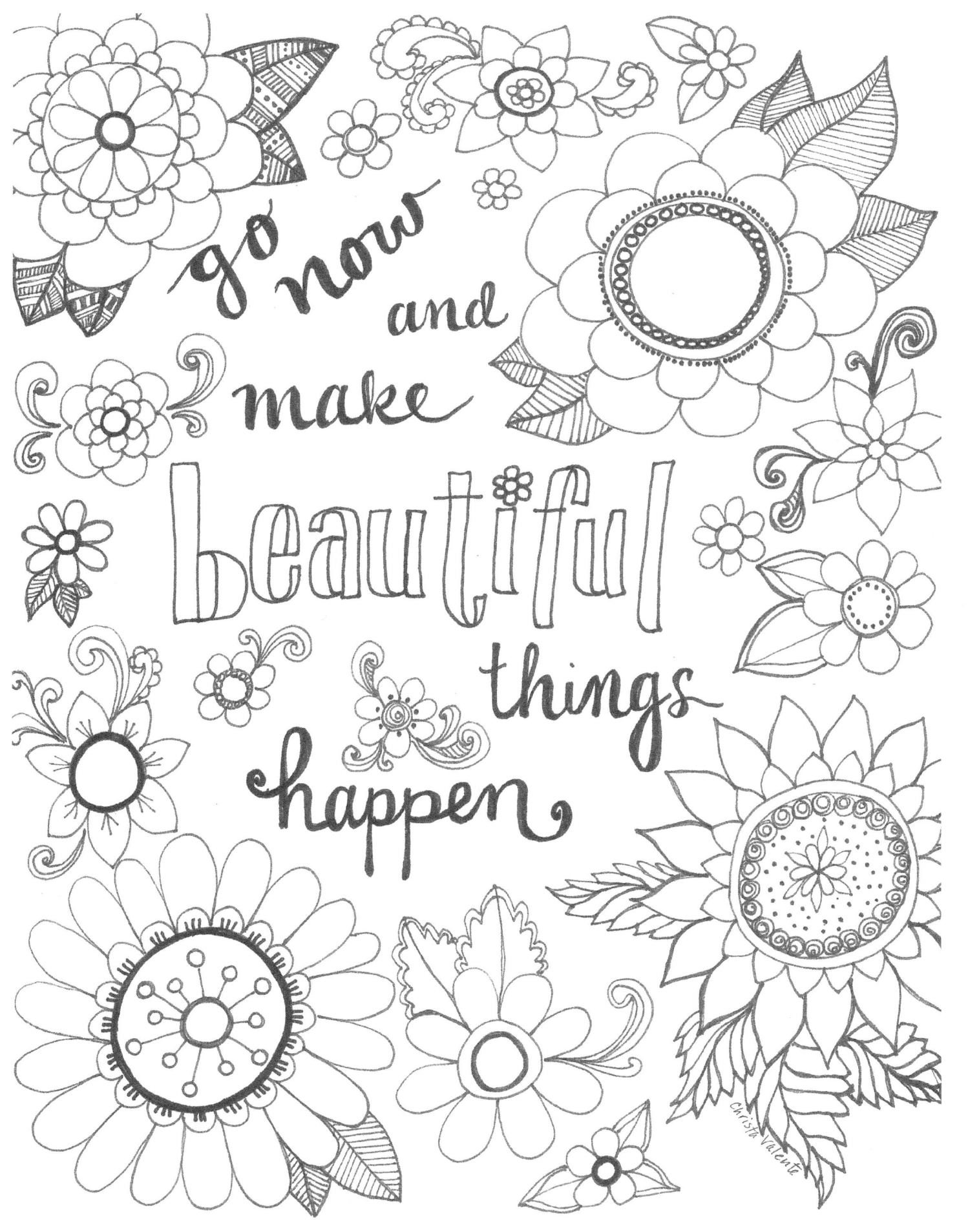